Contents

Words printed in **bold** are explained in the
glossary on pages 122-3

Most people think that **chaos** is just a mess. It's something that doesn't obey any rules.

You might think that nobody could explain chaos.

But, although chaos looks like a mess, it really does obey rules.

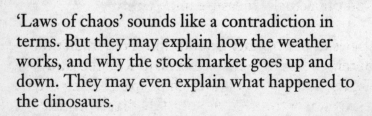

'Laws of chaos' sounds like a contradiction in terms. But they may explain how the weather works, and why the stock market goes up and down. They may even explain what happened to the dinosaurs.

Most people think that uncertainty is when you don't know something you ought to know. There is an answer, but you have forgotten it.

You might think that nobody could measure uncertainty.

STAY STILL!

But there are some things that are never certain. You can actually measure uncertainty.

'Laws of uncertainty' sounds like a contradiction in terms. But they help to explain why the **Sun** shines, and how computer chips work. They even explain how the laser in your CD player works.

5

What is chaos?

Something has to change for chaos to happen.

Things change
because
something
makes
them
change.

Chaos happens when a very tiny difference in the way you do something has a very big effect on what happens later.

This is called 'being sensitive to **initial conditions**'.

The fate of a raindrop can be very sensitive to where it falls. If it falls right near the top of a mountain range, but just on one side, it will get into a river that flows into one ocean.

I KNOW WHICH WAY I'D LIKE TO GO.

If the raindrop falls a few millimetres away, it
will end up in a different ocean, thousands of
miles away.

But you need more than this
to make chaos.

To make chaos out of falling water, the fate of the water drop has to have a big effect on something. This can happen in a certain kind of water wheel.

The buckets have holes in them, so they are constantly leaking as they go round.

When water flows in slowly, the weight of the full buckets makes the wheel go round the same way all the time. The buckets empty before they reach the bottom.

matter if we knew
flapping its wings.
ing that makes
nstant, in every day,
er exactly. But this

When the water is
flowing in quickly,
the buckets don't
ever get empty. The
wheel turns faster
and slower, and even
goes in the opposite
direction some of
the time. It behaves
chaotically. The
chaos, in this case,
depends on falling
drops of water.

One of the things that changes and is very
sensitive to initial conditions is the weather. A
little breezes add up to make winds. Winds p
clouds around and change where the rain fall

The Butterfly Effect wouldn't
exactly how every butterfly was
If we know exactly how everyth
breezes was working, at every i
then we could predict the weat
is impossible!

BUTTERFLY
FLAPS ITS
WINGS IN
BRAZIL

TODAY WILL BE
SUNNY IN PLACES
BECOMING
INCREASINGLY
CHAOTIC IN THE
AFTERNOON

The weather does obey very strict laws. But it is sensitive to initial conditions. We don't know the initial conditions exactly, because we can't look at everything in the whole world all the time. So we cannot use the laws to predict weather exactly. This is chaos.

What is uncertainty?

Scientific uncertainty is different from everyday uncertainty. When scientists talk about uncertainty, they know exactly what they mean. They can measure uncertainty.

Scientific uncertainty matters when we are dealing with tiny things like **atoms** and **electrons**.

Everything is made of atoms. Atoms are tiny. If you had ten million atoms side by side they would just stretch across the gap between two of the pointed bits on the edge of a stamp.

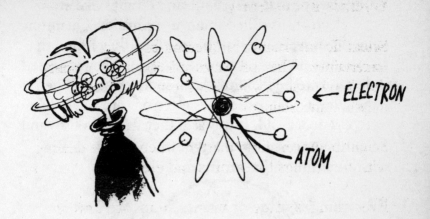

ELECTRON

ATOM

Atoms are made of even smaller things. There is a hard lump in the middle of the atom. This is called the **nucleus**. There are tiny particles whizzing round the outside of an atom. They are called electrons.

But there is something strange about electrons. They are not just hard lumps, like snooker balls. Somehow, they ripple, like waves on a pond.

This is where uncertainty comes from!

The science that deals with small things like atoms and electrons is called **quantum physics**. Quantum physicists were very surprised when they found that electrons are both wave and particle. They expected electrons to be like little hard snooker balls. Then they found that sometimes electrons are waves like ripples on a pond. It was as if they caught a fish, and found out that it was a tiger.

No one understands how this happens.
But it does.

You can see why the waviness of things like electrons makes them uncertain.

A wave is a spread out thing. You can never be certain about where a wave is. But you can say that the wave is inside something. Maybe it is inside your bath. It must be smaller than the thing it is inside. A wave inside your bath must be smaller than the bath, or it will slop out. So there is a way to measure quantum uncertainty.

A Brief History of Chaos and Uncertainty

You might think that history is all about chaos and uncertainty. Huge things like battles, plagues, famines and diseases seem to happen all the time, messing up everybody's lives, for trivial reasons. It's the butterfly effect again, making life very chaotic and uncertain.

There's a little rhyme that
sums up chaos
in history:

For the want of a Nail, a Shoe was lost
For the want of a Shoe, a Horse was lost
For the want of a Horse, a Rider was lost
For the want of a Rider, a Battle was lost
For the want of a Battle, a Kingdom was lost

The Ancient Greeks had some ideas about chaos. Eight hundred years before Jesus Christ was born, a Greek poet called Theogony wrote that

"first of all Chaos came to be."

They seem to have had the idea that the Universe was a complete mess to start with, and that sensible things like the Earth and people emerged out of this chaos, as if by magic (or because the gods made it happen).

But they didn't know why. That was about as far as any thinking about chaos went for the next 28 centuries.

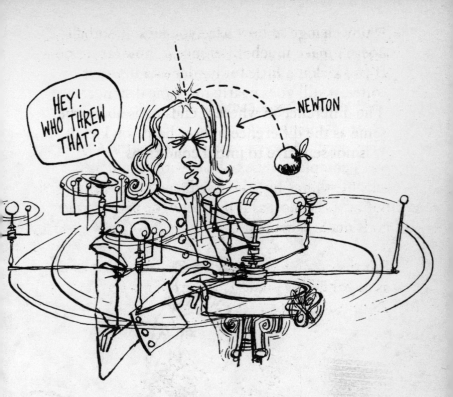

When science got started in the 17th century,
people like Galileo and Newton stuck to the
questions they could find answers for. They found
there were lots of things which obeyed simple laws
in a very predictable way. Things like the way the
planets move round the Sun.

A tiny change in how hard you kick a football doesn't make much difference to how far it goes. If you kick it a little bit harder or a little bit softer, it still goes nearly the same distance. The difference in where it ends up is about the same as the difference in how hard you kick it. It is not sensitive to initial conditions.

For more than two hundred years, from the time of Isaac Newton onwards, scientists didn't even try to think about complicated things that are sensitive to initial conditions. All the science from the 17th century to the 19th century dealt with things that are insensitive (like footballs). Things like clocks, the way the Moon moves round the Earth, how pistons work in steam engines. If you poked all these things that scientists were working on in those days gently, they wouldn't change very much.

PHARP

Isaac Newton worked out his law of **gravity** in the 17th century. It explains how the Sun holds on to a single planet by gravity, and keeps it in **orbit**. But unfortunately it is extremely hard to work out what happens if two (or more) planets are going round the Sun, because the gravity of each planet tugs on the other one. This might make them wander out of their orbits. Newton thought that from time to time God might have to push the planets back where they belong.

THE SUN

At the end of the 18th century, the Frenchman Pierre Laplace actually worked out the orbits of Jupiter and Saturn, the two biggest planets in our **Solar System**, together. Using Newton's laws, Laplace found that, although the planets sometimes wandered off a little bit from where Newton himself had said they ought to go, they always wandered back again after a few hundred years.

When Laplace wrote a book about his work, Napoleon Bonaparte read it. Napoleon asked Laplace why there was no mention of God in his book. Laplace proudly replied that he did not need God to explain how the planets moved.

THE KING OF SWEDEN

ER....JUST WHAT I'VE ALWAYS WANTED

MATHS COMPETITION

The first sign of chaos in science appeared in 1889 as a bizarre birthday present for Oscar II, King of Sweden and Norway.

For some strange reason, Swedish mathematicians decided to honour the King by organising a mathematics competition, with a big cash prize. One of the questions in the competition was how to prove that the entire Solar System really was stable, and that all the planets would stay in their orbits.

The prize was won by a Frenchman,
Henri Poincare. His answer had some good
news, and some bad news.

The good news is that the orbits of the planets
of the Solar System do have stable orbits.
The bad news is that this is only because the
Sun is so much bigger than the planets. Its
gravity overwhelms the nudges the planets
give each other.

OI!
WHO
ARE
YOU
SHOVING!?

Nobody took much notice of Poincare's discovery until the 1960s. Physicists were too busy inventing quantum physics (coming up soon) and relativity (explained in our book *Time and the Universe*).

It was Edward Lorenz, an American meteorologist, who discovered chaos at work here on Earth in 1961.

Lorenz used a computer to try to predict how weather would change. The computer used numbers for things like temperature and wind direction. He thought that if you changed the numbers you put in to the computer a little bit, the forecast you got out would change a little bit.

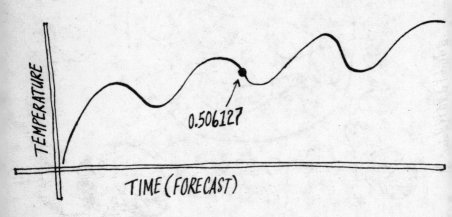

His computer was very slow compared to modern machines. One day, Lorenz wanted to extend one of his forecasts. Instead of running it from the beginning, he typed in the numbers from halfway through the first forecast, and started the machine in the middle of the calculation. He was amazed when the new forecast came out completely different.

Then he found out why. One of the numbers he typed in was 0.506. He hadn't bothered with the whole number – 0.506127. That tiny difference made a big change in the forecast. Weather is sensitive to initial conditions. Lorenz had discovered the Butterfly Effect.

The Butterfly Effect happens because you cannot be certain exactly how sensitive things start out. But this is different from the kind of uncertainty to do with quantum waves. As if one kind of uncertainty wasn't bad enough, scientists have two kinds of uncertainty to worry about.

Quantum uncertainty was only discovered in the 1920s. The person who discovered it was a German scientist called Werner Heisenberg, who was only 26 at the time. In 1927 he said,

"We cannot know, as a matter of principle, the present in all its details."

Quantum physics started exactly at the beginning of the 20th century, in the year 1900.

Before 1900, scientists were sure that light is a wave. They were sure because they had an experiment to prove it.

If you shine light through two tiny holes (or slits) on to a white screen in a dark room, it makes a pattern of light and shade. This is called an interference pattern. It is made by light waves spreading out from each hole, just like ripples on a pond, and overlapping. They interfere with one another.

So – light must be a wave.

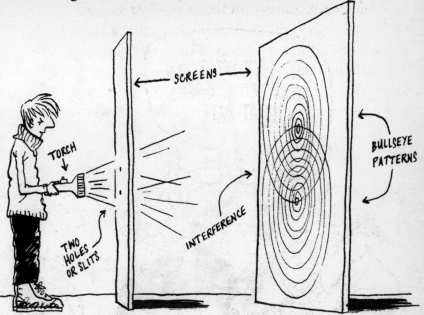

This drawing by Thomas Young (1773-1828) shows interference by alternate bright and dark lines. Try holding the right edge up to your eyes.

In 1900 a German scientist called Max Planck
made an amazing discovery. He found that
sometimes light does not behave like a wave.
It behaves like a stream of tiny particles,
little bullets.

The way Planck discovered this is hard to
understand. Even he wasn't sure what it meant.
But five years later Albert Einstein made it all
much clearer.

Einstein explained something called the **photoelectric effect**. This is when light hits a metal and makes electricity. It happens in solar powered radios and calculators.

If one colour of light hits the metal, it always knocks out electrons with the same energy from the electrons. If the light is faint, you just get a few electrons, but if the light is bright, you get lots. For the same colour of light, each electron has the same energy.

This is hard to explain if light is a wave. But it is easy to explain if light is like a stream of little bullets. Each little bullet carries the same amount of energy. When it hits the metal and knocks an electron out, the electron has the same energy as the 'bullet'.

But each colour of light has bullets with different energy.

The idea that light was both a wave and a particle was so amazing that it took years for scientists to work out what it meant. At first, each piece of light (each 'bullet') was called a quantum. Today, they are known as **photons**.

The most important thing about quantum physics was that it helped explain how atoms work. Niels Bohr, a Danish physicist, said that electrons must orbit round the nucleus in the middle, a bit like planets going round the Sun. An electron can only be in one orbit or another orbit. Light is made when an electron jumps from one orbit to another, and releases exactly one quantum of energy (one photon).

This is the famous 'quantum leap'.

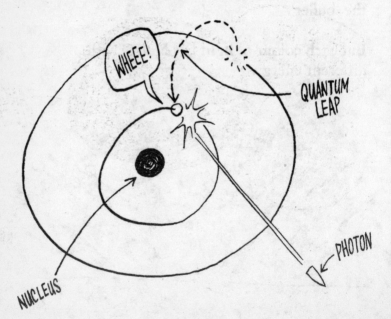

The important thing about a quantum jump is that there is nothing in between the two orbits.

The electron can only be in one orbit or the other, not halfway across. To an electron, there is no such place as 'halfway across'. It jumps instantly, without crossing the gap. It's like beaming up and beaming down in *Star Trek*.

This seems strange to us, because it is not what we are used to in everyday life. But it is perfectly normal if you are an electron.

WHO ARE YOU CALLING STRANGE?

HAVE YOU LOOKED IN THE MIRROR RECENTLY?

← ANGRY ELECTRON

When an electron jumps down inside an atom, it makes a photon. This is called emission. When a photon hits an atom, the electron jumps up and the photon is absorbed. Every atom has a different arrangement of electrons. The way they emit and absorb light makes different patterns of colours called a spectrum.

This is like a fingerprint for each element. It means you can work out what sorts of atoms things are made of just by looking very carefully at the colours of their light. Astronomers can even work out what stars are made of just by looking at starlight.

In 1916, Albert Einstein used the new quantum physics to predict a strange phenomenon. If the atoms in a crystal are given an energy boost, the electrons jump out further from the nucleus. They are called excited atoms.

EXCITED ATOMS

Usually, the electrons in excited atoms fall back in a haphazard way, making ordinary light. But Einstein worked out that if a single particle of light with exactly the right energy travelled through the crystal after it had been energised, the electrons would fall back together, like toppling dominoes.

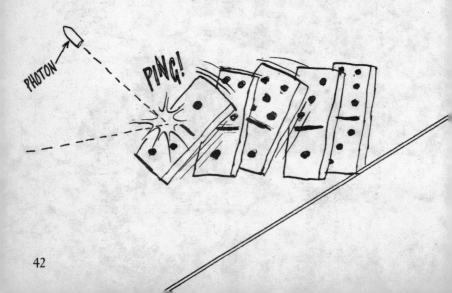

PHOTON

PING!

This would make a beam of intense light with a pure colour. This is called stimulated emission, and it is how a laser (the name comes from Light Amplification by Stimulated Emission of Radiation) works – although lasers were not made until forty years later, which just shows how clever Einstein was.

LASER

EINSTEIN

ZZZZ

AS IF THEY DIDN'T KNOW I WAS PRETTY SMART ALREADY

Physicists were so busy working out what it meant for light to be a wave and a particle that it wasn't until 1923 that someone asked the question,

"What if an electron is both a particle and a wave?"

Now this idea seems obvious, but no one had thought of it before.

The person who asked the question was a French nobleman, Prince Louis-Victor Pierre Raymond de Broglie. He was quite old for a scientist (over 30) when he came up with the idea, because his career had been interrupted by World War One. In the war, he worked in the army on radio communication, and he was stationed in Paris at the Eiffel Tower, which was used as a big radio aerial.

GREAT SOUND!

One of the people who tested de Broglie's idea was
George Thomson, a British physicist. In 1927 he
did experiments with electrons that showed they
could interfere with one another like ripples on a
pond. De Broglie was right!

George Thomson got the Nobel Prize in 1937 for
proving that electrons are waves. His father,
J. J. Thomson (always known by his initials) had
won the Nobel Prize 31 years earlier for proving
that electrons are particles.

Both of then were right. Both deserved the Prize.
This is a perfect example of how weird the quantum
world is.

The person who put all of these ideas together in 1927 and found the equations that describe quantum uncertainty was Werner Heisenberg, in Germany.

Heisenberg was already famous for his work in quantum physics. He had some of his best ideas in 1925, when he had such a fierce attack of hayfever that he had to go to the rocky island of Heligoland to recover. When he arrived, his face was so puffed up that his landlady thought he had been beaten up. But when he got better, there was nothing to do on the island except think about science.

HEISENBERG

HELIGOLAND

You might think that this extra uncertainty makes chaos worse. But here's a strange thing. The way atoms absorb energy shows that there is *less* chaos when quantum effects are important. This is because of the way waves interfere. Because 'points' are blurred out by quantum uncertainty, it isn't quite so crucial to say what the initial conditions are. This doesn't help when we are dealing with things bigger than atoms. But it does mean we won't need to worry about quantum uncertainty for the rest of this book!

POINTS → . . (NO INTERFERENCE)

FUZZY → 🟤🟤 (INTERFERENCE)
BLOBS

Uncertainty turns points into fuzzy blobs. This means they interfere with each other more easily. It doesn't matter so much exactly where the points are.

SO WHAT'S YOUR POINT?

Getting a Grip on Chaos

Even if something is very sensitive to initial conditions, you might think that if you had a powerful enough computer you could say what the initial conditions were accurately enough to tame chaos. You would be able to predict exactly everything that was going to happen.

But this doesn't happen.

Think of a line 1 metre long. There are lots of points along the line that you can label with fractions – the point $\frac{1}{2}$ way along, $\frac{3}{4}$ the way along, and so on. (Remember that 1 cm is $\frac{1}{100}$ of a metre, so measuring in centimetres is measuring in fractions).

$$\pi = 3.141592\ldots$$

If you are specifying the position of anything, that is an initial condition. Some initial conditions can only be specified as **irrational numbers**. For example, the position of 'you choose – anything you like!' So if things are really sensitive to initial conditions, chaos is inevitable.

Numbers you can write as fractions of whole numbers are called **rational numbers**, because they are ratios. A ratio is one whole number divided by another whole number.

But there are some numbers that cannot be written as ratios of two whole numbers. They correspond to numbers like pi, with an infinite number of numbers after the decimal point. Pi is a number that goes on forever. It starts out 3.14159, but there is no end to the numbers after the decimal point. There are lots of numbers like pi that go on forever. They are called irrational numbers because they are not ratios.

There are points on the line (any line) that correspond to irrational numbers. There is a point, for example, exactly pi centimetres along the line from its end. If you want to say exactly where that point is, you need an infinite number of numbers.

$\frac{3}{4}$ 1

To say exactly where just one point on a line is, you would need a computer bigger than the entire Universe!

3589793238462643383279502884197169399375105

DID SOMEONE MENTION PIE?

RUMBLE RUMBLE

If one ice cream costs £1, then if I have twice as much money (£2) I can buy twice as many ice creams (two). With £5 I can buy five times as many ice creams, and so on. This is called a **linear** pattern. The problem with chaos is that it is **nonlinear**. If something is linear, whatever you do in the beginning has the same size effect at the end.

If the way money worked was nonlinear, perhaps if I had £2 I could get four of the ice creams that cost £1 each, and if I had £3 I could buy eight of them, and so on. This is a nonlinear sequence.

Some special offers in supermarkets are a bit nonlinear – like three for the price of two. But you never see eight for the price of three – that really would cause chaos!

When you stride down the street, each step might go 1 metre. After ten steps, you have gone 10 metres. Walking is linear.

If you had magic boots, each step could be twice as big as the one before. The first, 1 metre; the next, 2 metres; the third, 4 metres; and so on.

After the first two steps, each step is bigger than all the steps that went before put together. The eleventh step on its own would be more than a kilometre. The magic boots are nonlinear.

2 metres

2 metres

Dropping stones from a bridge is linear. If you move 2 metres to the left before you drop the stone, it falls into the river 2 metres to the left, and so on.

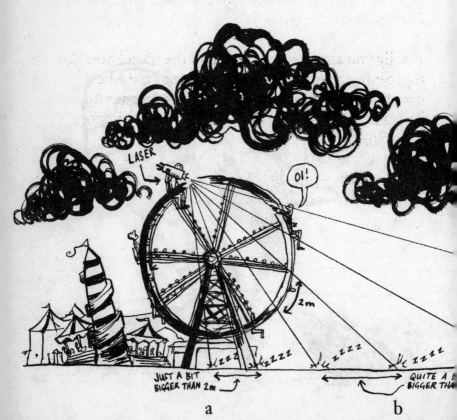

LASER

OI!

2m

ZZZZ   ZZZZ   ZZZZ   ZZZZ

JUST A BIT
BIGGER THAN 2m

QUITE A [
BIGGER THA

a   b

But suppose you shine a powerful laser beam from the top of a big wheel, with a rule that the beam must go through two points on the wheel, each 2 metres apart.

You start by aiming nearly straight down. In this case, moving the point 2 metres around the wheel doesn't make much difference to where the beam shines. Two adjacent spots of laser light will not be much more than 2 metres apart when they hit the ground (a).

Then you aim the beam further up the wheel. Shifting the point 2 metres around the wheel now makes a bigger difference to where adjacent spots of laser light hit the ground (b).

Finally you aim the beam through the wheel near the top. Shifting the point 2 metres around the wheel now has a huge effect on where the beam ends up. Two adjacent spots of laser light will be much more than 2 metres apart (c).

This system is sometimes nearly linear, and sometimes nonlinear. Sometimes it is not chaotic, and sometimes it is.

Confusing, isn't it? That's chaos for you!

← HUGELY BIGGER THAN 2 m →

c

You can see a system that changes from being linear to being chaotic in your own home. Try turning the cold tap on in the bath, very gently.

If you turn the tap on a little bit, the water flows out smoothly and gently.

Now turn the tap on as far as it will go.

If you turn the tap open all the way, the water gushes out all over the place (this kind of chaos is called turbulence).

TURBULENCE

If you are very careful, you may be able to get the water flowing in an in-between way, with regular ripples wobbling it about. We'll have more to say about the region between linearity and chaos later. (Don't worry if you can't get your water rippling like this; it is quite hard to do!)

If you don't like getting wet, try chaos in a calculator.

Start with a mathematical expression, $(2x^2 - 1)$. Then do something called **iteration**. Iteration means doing the same thing over and over again. Put any number you like (between 0 and 1) into the calculator, square it, multiply by 2, and take away 1. Do the same thing with the number you end up with, and so on.

Try it for different numbers. Write down the series of numbers you get, for ten iterations. You might guess that a tiny change in the number you start with won't make much difference in the numbers at each stage of the iteration.

Try it with 0.51234, and then with 0.51235.

That's chaos!

Don't be surprised if you get different numbers doing the same trick on different calculators. It's because they round off the decimals inside differently, like Lorenz's weather forecast.

This is a VERY IMPORTANT DISCOVERY.

All computers round off numbers. They do it in different ways. So the same program run on two different computers can give different answers!

Computers are not perfect, and they do not always even agree with each other. You shouldn't believe things just because 'the computer says so.' Find out WHY the computer says so!

OH, FAIR
ENOUGH

WITHDRAWALS

fig 1

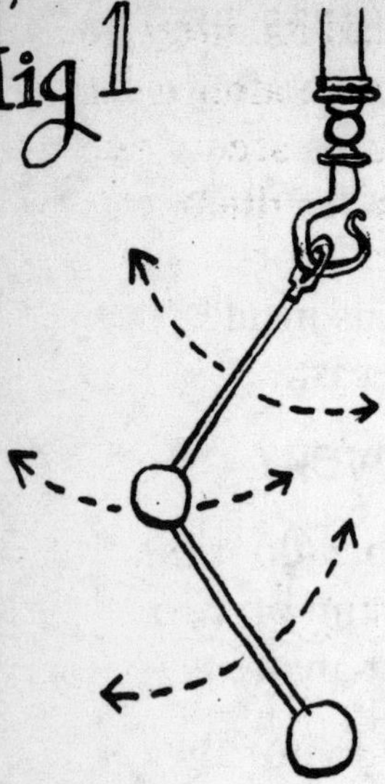

There is a very simple thing that shows chaos at work. It is a kind of double pendulum made of two rods, usually the same length as each other, joined by a hinge. Like an ordinary pendulum, the double pendulum can swing to and fro from its top, as well as having the hinge in the middle.

If you give the double pendulum a push, it doesn't just swing back and forth like an ordinary single pendulum.

fig 2

Sometimes, the bottom rod swings from side to side while the top rod hardly moves (fig.1).

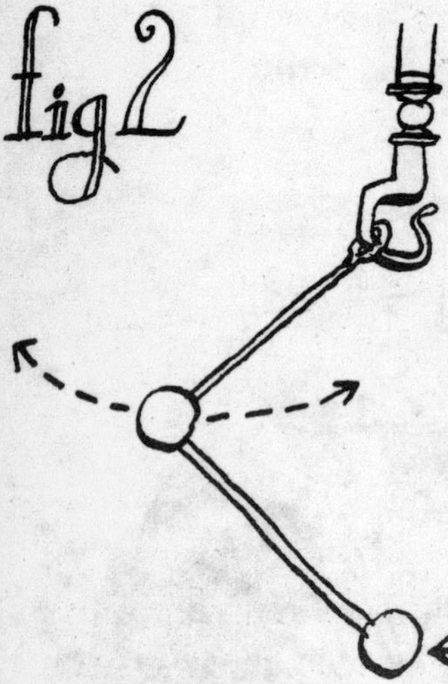

Sometimes, the hinge between the two rods swings to and fro while the top of the top rod and the bottom of the bottom rod hardly move (fig.2).

← DOESN'T MOVE SIDEWAYS — ONLY UP & DOWN

Sometimes, the two rods swing together as if there were no hinge in the middle (fig.3).

The double pendulum goes through all its different kinds of motion while it is slowing down after it has been pushed. (Some of these pendulums are jiggled about by a little electric motor that gives them a nudge from time to time.)

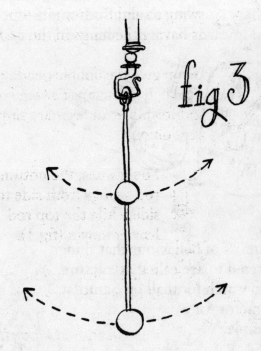

fig 3

For a while, the double pendulum swings one way. But as it slows to a critical speed, or is given a tiny nudge, a tiny change in its speed makes it start swinging in a different way.

Complicated systems behave as if they were attracted towards some patterns of behaviour.

Actually, even simple things behave like this, but it is so obvious we don't think about it.

An ordinary single pendulum behaves as if it were attracted towards swinging backwards and forwards.

YOU MAY THINK IT'S A BORING LIFE. BUT I FIND IT RATHER ATTRACTIVE

The patterns of behaviour that things are attracted to are called **attractors**. Going to watch football on Saturday is an attractor for a lot of people.

Having attractors also tells us about a lot of things that cannot happen. Flags never point into the wind. The temperature in the heart of the Brazilian rainforest never falls below freezing. There are no attractors for that kind of behaviour in the rules that describe how flags flap, or the rules that describe how the weather machine works.

In chaotic systems, there are attractors so powerful that they don't allow any other pattern of behaviour (it's as if you HAVE to go to the football on Saturday, and you don't have any choice). But there are several of these attractors. So something like the double pendulum has to change suddenly from one pattern to another one. It can't do anything in between.

It's as if some Saturdays you HAVE to go to the football, and some Saturdays you HAVE to wash the car, but you can NEVER go to the pictures on Saturday. These would be rigid rules that could never be broken.

It's a bit like having a rule which says that on 1 August every year, the midday temperature in London must be either exactly 20°C, or 30°C, but it can never be anything else.

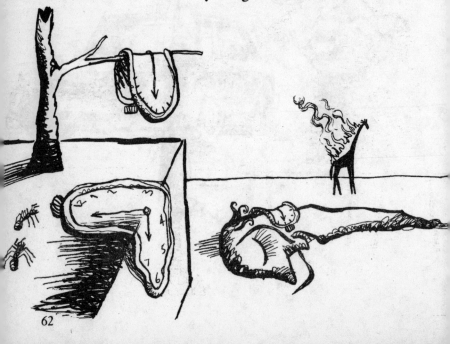

This is a bit strange. So chaotic attractors are called **strange attractors**. But there really isn't anything strange about chaotic attractors. What's strange is the way that chaos flips a system from one attractor to another, with nothing in between (almost like the quantum jump).

And even that only seems strange because it isn't what we are used to in everyday life. It's perfectly normal, as far as the Universe is concerned.

The way strange attractors relate to one another is a bit like a thing called the Cantor set.

Georg Cantor invented set theory more than a hundred years ago. But Henry Smith invented the Cantor set in 1875. Cantor didn't use it until 1883. Perhaps mathematicians thought the name 'Smith set' would be boring.

You make a Cantor set by starting with a line. Rub out the middle third of the line, but leave its end points. Then rub out the middle thirds of the two lines that are left, and so on.

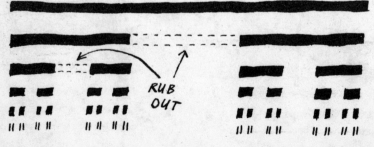

Eventually, you are left with nothing but the points which were the end points of all the lines you rubbed out. There is lots of empty space, with little clusters of points here and there along it. This is sometimes called Cantor dust.

You can make a more complicated pattern of dust by having a more complicated rule for rubbing out bits of the lines. And you can make the dust in three dimensions, by starting with a block of stuff and nibbling out pieces, making it like a Swiss cheese.

Nobody ever actually does this. It's all described by maths, so you don't have to actually nibble at cheeses. It turns out that the way chaotic attractors are arranged is rather like a complicated Cantor dust.

Chaos wouldn't be so chaotic if all the points corresponding to attractors stayed in order along the line, even if they were spread out like dust. There might be a rule that the temperature could only be an even number of degrees, but as you went along the line it would still jump neatly from 20 to 22 to 24 and so on.

But usually the attractors are jumbled up. A way to picture this jumbling is by looking at how some kinds of layered pastry are made.

First, you stretch the dough one way. Then, you fold it over and squash it flat. Stretch, fold and squeeze as often as you like. Two places that start next to each other in the dough end up far apart. Two places that start out far apart may end up next to each other.

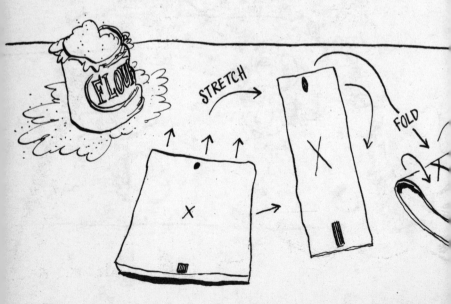

Chaos is like that. The attractor 'next door' might not be the one you expect from common sense. If it really was chaotic, the temperature might jump from 20° to 48°, then to 26°, then to 12°, up to 30°, and so on. There would seem to be no pattern to it, even though you were moving steadily along the line of points in the Cantor dust. Next door attractors might correspond to completely different patterns of behaviour.

YEAH, YEAH... BUT WHEN DO WE EAT?

SQUASH

STRETCH

etc. etc. etc......

One of the most important things about the Cantor set is that if you zoom in on any bit of it, it looks exactly the same as the whole thing.

Anywhere you zoom in to, you will find a line. Every line gets divided up by the same rule – take out the middle third, and so on.

There is no end to the pattern, and every bit of the pattern looks exactly like the whole pattern. It is said to be 'self-similar'.

This is called a fractal. Chaotic attractors usually make fractal patterns, but they are much more complicated than the simple Cantor dust pattern.

Fractals make pretty patterns (a snowflake is a kind of fractal). But this is all you really need to know about fractals – they make exactly the same pattern, no matter how much you zoom in on them. Scientists say they are the same on all scales, or 'scale free'.

There's a nice example of **self-similarity** that most of us have seen. In some tourist villages, they have a model of the village, big enough for you to walk round.

In the model village, at the place corresponding to where the model is, you will find a model of the model. And in the model of the model, there will be a model of the model of the model.

The models usually stop there. But you can imagine them going on forever, with each model a perfect copy of the whole thing.

There's a little rhyme about self-similarity.

> Big fleas have little fleas,
> upon their backs to bite 'em.
> And little fleas have smaller fleas,
> and so ad infinitum.

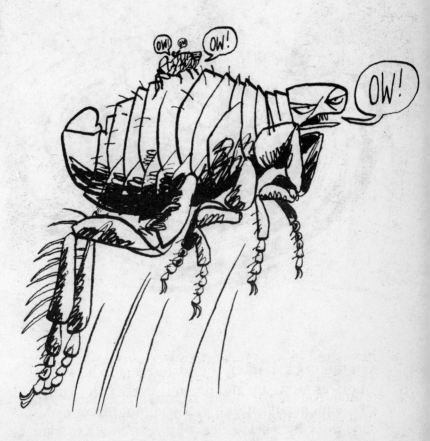

Of course, real fleas aren't fractal.

Things being self-similar in chaos means that things that look quite messy to us actually have a repeating pattern inside them. In turbulence, each swirl of water (or air) has identical smaller swirls inside it, and each smaller swirl is filled with even smaller swirls, and so on.

On the stock market, the pattern made by a graph of prices going up and down is exactly the same, mathematically speaking, if you plot prices day by day, week by week, or year by year. Stock market fluctuations are self-similar. They are governed by the same rules as chaos.

The reason people took so long to understand chaos wasn't just because they were busy doing quantum physics. Because you can't find simple answers to the equations that describe chaos, you have to work each step out on a computer. Computers only got good enough to do this in the 1980s.

Modern weather forecasting was invented by Lewis Fry Richardson in 1922. He worked out that 64,000 mathematicians, each working a mechanical adding machine, could make a forecast for tomorrow's weather before tomorrow came. A computer as good as 64,000 mathematicians with adding machines wasn't invented until the 1950s.

That's enough maths to be going on with.

Now we know a bit about chaos, let's take another look at what goes on in the Solar System.

If you have three or more bodies orbiting around each other, the motion can sometimes be regular and periodic. This means that each orbit goes round and round the same track, and always takes the same time, in the same way as the Earth always takes a year to go once round the Sun.

But sometime the orbits are chaotic. It depends where you are, and how big you are.

Remember Henri Poincare (page 29)? He found that if you try to work out the orbits for three or more planets, all roughly the same size, going round each other (without a Sun), then there are no stable orbits. Two planets go round each other in the same boring orbits forever. But if a third one is there, the orbits get jumbled up, with the planets whizzing about in all kinds of weird orbits. The 'three body problem' has no answer.

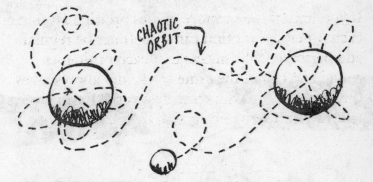

CHAOTIC ORBIT

If you have two big bodies going round each other, and one tiny body trying to orbit round both of them, chaos only affects the little one. This is much more like the way things are in the Solar System. The big Sun and the (fairly big) planets behave sensibly. Little bits of stuff sometimes behave sensibly and sometimes don't.

A good place to see the result of chaos in the Solar System is in the rings of Saturn. Saturn is a planet that is much bigger than the Earth and further away from the Sun than we are. It has lots of moons going round it, and also a set of rings.

The rings are made up of millions of tiny pieces of ice and rock, each one like a miniature moon in orbit around the planet. The only things that have much effect on the orbits of these mini-moons is the gravity of Saturn (because it is so close) and the gravity of the Sun (because it is so big).

MINI MOON

GAP

RING

There are gaps in the rings because some orbits are affected by chaos. They are unstable. Any mini-moon that wanders into one of those orbits soon gets flung off into space.

THWACK

CHAOS

SATURN →

The rings of Saturn are a long way away, and what happens there doesn't much matter to us.

But there is chaos at work much closer to home in the Solar System, and it might be very important for life on Earth.

To see why, we need to know what the Solar System is like.

The Sun is at the middle of the Solar System. It is a star, and has 99.86 per cent of all the mass in the Solar System.

Working outward from the Sun there are four rocky planets – Mercury, Venus, Earth and Mars. Then there is a belt of cosmic rubble, like the rings of Saturn but much bigger. Outside this **asteroid** belt there are four gassy planets – Jupiter, Saturn, Uranus and Neptune. Jupiter has twice as much mass as all the other planets put together.

There's another object that is usually called a planet (Pluto), but this is only a small lump of icy stuff, not a real planet.

The interesting things to look at to find chaos at work are the rocks of the asteroid belt. Some of them are only pebbles, but some are tens of kilometres across.

The orbits of rocks in the asteroid belt are only affected by the gravity of the Sun (which has a strong influence because it is very big) and the gravity of Jupiter (which is not as big as the Sun but is much closer to the asteroids).

There are gaps in the asteroid belt, like the gaps in Saturn's rings. They are there for the same reason – chaos.

In some cases an asteroid can spend 100,000 years orbiting round in the belt before suddenly being flung into an orbit diving closer to the Sun. You have to calculate 100,000 years worth of orbits before anything interesting happens. This was done in 1981.

If there was nothing else to worry about, the rock could just as suddenly get flipped back into its old orbit.

But there is something else to worry about. The temporary orbit of the asteroid may take it past Mars. It may crash into Mars, or the gravity of Mars might swing it right round and send it out into space. Jupiter (and chaos) pass the asteroid to Mars, and Mars gets rid of it.

Some asteroids get past Mars and hit the Earth. The dinosaurs were wiped out by an asteroid which hit 65 million years ago. Chaos in the asteroid belt really does affect life on Earth.

It's time we took a closer look at what life is all about.

JUPITER

Life on the Edge of Chaos

Life is very complicated. It is also complex. When scientists say something is complex, they mean that lots of bits work together to make something interesting. They are organised so they work together. A single wheel is not very complex. A bicycle is.

One of the big puzzles in science is where complex things come from. If complex things are left alone, usually they fall to bits and get disorganised. Things wear out. This is all to do with the **Second Law of Thermodynamics** and the arrow of time, which we explained in our book *Time and the Universe*.

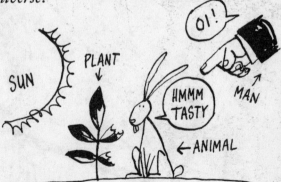

The important discovery, made long before chaos theory, is that complex things exist where they can feed off a flow of energy. Life on Earth, for example, feeds off the flow of energy from the Sun.

When energy flows in the right way, things get organised into patterns all by themselves. This is called self-organization.

There is a very simple experiment that shows self-organization.

(WARNING: DON'T TRY THIS AT HOME!)

If a shallow pan of oily liquid is warmed from underneath, at first the heat travels upward by conduction. The heat travels through the liquid, but the liquid doesn't move. As it gets hotter, the liquid at the bottom of the pan starts to rise. This is called convection. At first, the convection is messy. Then it settles into a beautiful layer of hexagonal convection cells, with hot liquid rising up the sides of the cells and cool liquid falling down in the middle of each cell.

A simple pile of sand is a good example of self-organization at work.

A heap of sand on a table just sits there and does nothing. It is stable and boring.

If lots of sand is poured on to the table all the time, the pile of sand is constantly changing in chaotic ways and no interesting patterns stay there for long.

But if grains of sand are dropped on to the table slowly, they pile up until they reach a critical point. This happens when the slope of the sand 'hill' makes a certain angle. At that point, adding a single grain of sand makes avalanches all over the pile (some big, some small) and sand falls off the edge of the table. If a lot falls off, it takes a while for the pile to build up again. But on average, over a long time, for every grain of sand you add, just one grain falls off the table.

In this state, the pile of sand makes interesting patterns that stay for a while, then change suddenly because of avalanches. It is in a critical state, because the amount of sand falling off matches the amount falling on. The angle of the sand hill slope stays the same. This is called **self-organized criticality**. It only happens if you are putting something in from outside (in this case, falling grains of sand).

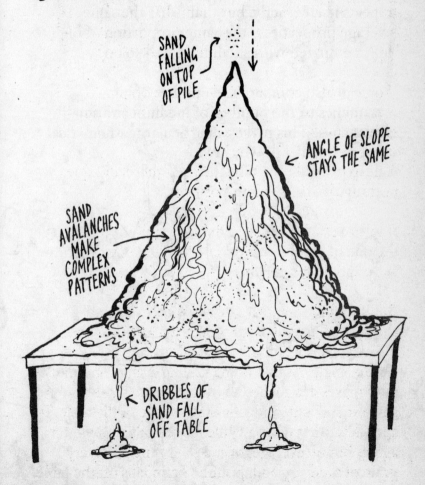

SAND FALLING ON TOP OF PILE

ANGLE OF SLOPE STAYS THE SAME

SAND AVALANCHES MAKE COMPLEX PATTERNS

DRIBBLES OF SAND FALL OFF TABLE

When sand is dropped at random over the table, not just in one place, it makes a pattern of hills and valleys. On average, when one grain is added one falls off the edge, because the sand is in a self-organised critical state.

In this critical state, the pattern of hills and valleys is self-similar. It has the same geometry wherever you zoom in. Thus doesn't mean the pattern repeats itself exactly, but that it has the same average properties – the same proportion of big hills compared with small hills, and so on.

You can also compare the number of big avalanches to the number of medium and small avalanches. This makes a particular mathematical pattern called a **power law**.

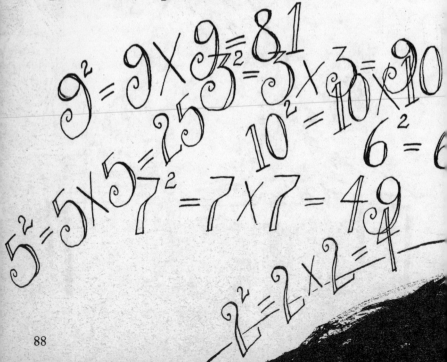

In maths, 'power' means the number of times you multiply something by itself. 4^2 means 4 x 4 and is also '4 to the power of 2'. A power law is one where changing one number changes another number by a certain power. For example, doubling one number might mean you have to multiply another number by itself.

The exciting thing about all this is that the same mathematical pattern corresponding to self-organized criticality is found in the real world, in earthquakes, economics, and the evolution of life.

In the sandpile, adding a single grain of sand might trigger a small avalanche, or a big avalanche, or a lot of small avalanches, or any combination of large and small (and medium) avalanches. The same small trigger can have different-sized effects. This is because the sandpile is on the edge of chaos.

In the real world, the number of earthquakes with different sizes (called magnitudes) is like this. For every 1000 earthquakes with magnitude 4, there are 100 earthquakes with magnitude 5, 10 with magnitude 6, and so on. (By the way, an earthquake with magnitude 5 is ten times bigger than magnitude 4, 6 is ten times bigger than 5, and so on.) This is a power law.

STILL, WE OUGHT TO BE SAFE FOR A WHILE NOW....

Scientists used to think that you needed a big trigger to make a big earthquake. That would mean big earthquakes only happen after strain has built up in the rocks for many years. But now it seems that earthquakes behave like sandpiles. A small trigger could set off earthquakes of any size at all, it's just that small earthquakes happen more often.

This is amazing. Among other things, it means that if a big 'quake happened last year, you are not necessarily safe for a long time. In earthquake zones, any size earthquake could happen at any time.

RUMBLE RUMBLE

It is strange to think that economics might follow the same rule as sandpiles and earthquakes. But some scientists think it does.

Economics is all about money and banks and business. People buy shares in businesses in the stock market. The price of shares sometimes goes up and sometimes goes down. When it goes down a lot, it is called a 'stock market crash'.

Perhaps chaos is why stock market fluctuations are self-similar. Maybe the economy is in a self-organised critical state. If so, if the government tried to interfere (perhaps by trying to stop prices going up so much), it will eventually cause a big "avalanche" somewhere else in the economy. But these are very new ideas and nobody is quite sure yet what practical use they may have.

OH THIS IS CHAOS!

Traffic jams on crowded motorways also obey the same rules as the sandpile. The number of traffic jams of different sizes matches the power law. There are little jams inside big jams, and so on. And although sometimes big jams are caused by big effects, like a crash, sometimes a big jam on a crowded road can be caused just by one car slowing down a bit, or changing lane suddenly, and making the car behind brake, and so on down the line. Self-organised criticality really is all around us.

People think that the most important thing in the Universe is – people.

So how did we get to be here?

One of the most important reasons why we are here is that something killed off the dinosaurs about 65 million years ago. With no dinosaurs around, our ancestors were able to flourish and evolve (eventually) into us, and lots of other animals.

The dinosaurs, and many other animals and plants that were alive on Earth at the time, were killed when a lump of rock from space hit the Earth. The impact released as much energy as 100 million large nuclear bombs and devastated the environment of the planet. The place where it happened has been identified, in what is now the Yucatan Peninsula of Mexico. This disaster for life is called a **Mass Extinction**.

The lump of rock that caused the Mass Extinction almost certainly came from the asteroid belt.

We owe our existence to chaos in the Solar System.

But there is more.

The Mass Extinction in which the dinosaurs died wasn't the only one. Geologists know which species were alive long ago from the fossils preserved in the rocks. They know when those plants and animals were alive because they know how old the layers of rocks are. There have been lots of extinctions going back hundreds of millions of years.

Some extinctions are big, like the one in which the dinosaurs died.

Some extinctions are small, with only a few species dying out.

Some extinctions are medium-sized.

If you compare the numbers of extinctions of different size that occur in the fossil record, what do you find?

You guessed – it's a power law.

There are only 79 measured extinctions covering 600 million years. Some scientists think this is not enough to be sure they obey a power law. But if they do, it means that extinctions are self-similar. It means they behave like sandpiles and traffic jams. It means that even a small effect may produce a Mass Extinction, or just a small extinction, or something in between. To see how, we need to see how evolution works.

Charles Darwin explained evolution in terms of natural selection. There are two important things about evolution by natural selection.

← DARWIN

First, the offspring of plants and animals are similar to their parents, but not exactly the same as their parents. There are slight differences between individuals.

FATHER'S EARS

MOTHER'S NOSE

Secondly, there is competition between individuals for things like food or a chance to mate. So the individuals that are better suited to their surroundings do best and have more offspring. In Darwin's words, they are best 'fitted' to survive. (Survival of the fittest doesn't necessarily mean physical fitness, like athletes. It's more like the way a piece fits in to a jigsaw puzzle.)

So a small change that makes an individual better fitted means it leaves more offspring, who are enough like the parent to inherit that small change. Very slowly, this makes species better and better fitted to their environment.

One of the most important things that keeps Darwinian evolution going is – evolution itself.

Imagine a kind of frog that lives by catching flies on its sticky tongue. If some of the flies change slightly (evolve) and become more slippery, they don't get eaten. They thrive and have lots of slippery children.

But now, if a frog evolves with an extra sticky tongue, it will catch lots more flies than other frogs. It will thrive and have lots of children. The sticky tongue will be inherited by its descendants. Soon most frogs will have extra sticky tongues and most flies will be extra slippery.

VERY SMUG FROG

In the end, just as many frogs eat just as many flies. Both end up back where they started, even though they are evolving like mad. This is called the '**Red Queen effect**', because the Red Queen in *Alice Through the Looking Glass* by Lewis Carroll has to run as fast as she can to stay in the same place.

Even though frogs eat flies, frogs and flies do not compete with one another. Flies compete with other flies to escape, and slipperiness made these flies better fitted than smooth flies. Frogs compete with other frogs for food, and sticky-tongued frogs are better fitted than not-so-sticky-tongued frogs.

In the real world, frogs don't only eat flies, and flies have to worry about lots of other things besides frogs. Many species are affected by many other species, and also by changes in the world around them. This is called the environment. Living things and the environment affect each other, because they interact with each other. This complex web of interacting species and things is called an **ecology**. It exists on the edge of chaos. If a small change occurs (like flies becoming more slippery), it might only have a small effect on the ecology, or a medium sized effect, or a big effect. Evolution obeys the same rules as the sandpile. It is an example of self-organized criticality at work.

THERE GOES MY LUNCH!

HEH HEH

FLY ESCAPES

Suppose the flies became so good at escaping that the frogs starve. Now, the fish that live on the frogs' tadpoles starve. Bears that fed on the fish go hungry, and start to eat rabbits instead.

Just one small change in the ecology can make a ripple effect that spreads outwards to affect many other species. Perhaps it could cause an extinction which could be seen in the fossil record.

Even if dinosaurs were killed by a big rock from space (a meteorite), sometimes a small rock from space could have just as big an effect on life. Or some other change – a drought, or a big volcanic eruption, or just a change caused by evolution itself – could cause an extinction.

The pattern in the fossil record is just like the sandpile pattern. Things stay the same for a long time, then change quickly, then stay the same for a long time again, and so on. This happens to the whole ecology, and sometimes to individual species even when there is no big extinction. In evolution, it is called **Punctuated Equilibrium**.

NO, SORRY—
I CAN'T COME
OVER TONIGHT.
I'M EXTINCT

But it all depends on just what you mean by
'quickly'. Geologists looking at layers of rock are
lucky if they can tell the time more accurately than
about a hundred thousand years. One layer of rock
might be about 1.2 million years old, and the one
just above might be 1.1 million years old.

Punctuated Equilibrium doesn't mean that a species changes dramatically from one generation to the next. It isn't like a bird laying an egg which hatches out to become a mouse.

Evolutionary changes are still slow by human timescales.

If it took 12,000 generations for a mouse to evolve into a supermouse as big as an elephant, the change from one generation to the next would be too small to notice. A baby mouse would just grow up to be $\frac{1}{12,000}$ th bigger than its parents. If each generation took five years (somewhere in between the actual lifetimes of mice and elephants), the change would take 60,000 years. But in fossil terms, that is too quick to measure.

Dating fossils even 100,000 years apart is almost impossible. So in the fossil record you would jump straight from mouse to supermouse, as if a mouse had given birth to an elephant, even though the change is really quite slow. It is only quick compared with geological time.

Let's get back to the idea of life at the edge of chaos. It ties in with another Big Idea in science, called the **Gaia Hypothesis**.

The Gaia Hypothesis says that the whole Earth is like a single living organism, and the way life behaves helps to keep the planet suitable for life.

The name comes from the Greek goddess of the Earth, Gaia. People sometimes just say 'Gaia' as shorthand for 'the Gaia Hypothesis.'

The important thing about Gaia is **feedback**.
Here's an example.

When the Earth was young, the atmosphere was
rich in carbon dioxide. It helped to keep the world
warm, like a blanket round the planet. This was a
good thing, because the Sun was cooler then.
Without the warming effect of the carbon dioxide,
the world would have frozen.

As the Sun warmed up, Earth got hotter. Plants
flourished, and breathed in carbon dioxide,
weakening the warming effect. This kept the
temperature just right for life. If the plants took
too much carbon dioxide out of the air, the world
cooled, and some plants died, so the carbon
dioxide increased again and the world warmed.
This is feedback.

The Gaia Hypothesis was thought up by Jim Lovelock, when he was a consultant for NASA in the 1960s.

His job was to design instruments to go on space probes that would land on Mars. The instruments were supposed to look for signs of life.

One day, Lovelock realised that it was a waste of time. The atmosphere of Mars is made of carbon dioxide, which is a very stable, unreactive substance. It is stable and uninteresting in the same way that a pile of sand is stable and uninteresting if no more sand is being dropped on to it.

If Mars is so stable, he said, it cannot be a home for life.

Lovelock said that you could tell Mars was a dead planet even without going there. He said that putting his instruments on the Mars probes was as pointless as designing an automatic rover vehicle to cross the Sahara desert and then fitting it out with a fishing rod to catch the fish that live in the sand dunes.

This didn't make him popular at NASA, and they sent the space probes anyway. They didn't find any signs of life.

But the Earth is different. The atmosphere is rich in oxygen. Oxygen is a dangerous gas. It reacts violently with lots of things.

We don't think oxygen is dangerous because we are used to it. But even the way we use oxygen to make energy in our muscles is a form of slow burning. If the amount of oxygen in the air increased just a little bit, there would be huge forest fires until the level dropped again. This may have happened lots of times in the past – another example of feedback.

If there were no life on Earth (plants making oxygen out of carbon dioxide), all the oxygen would quickly be used up in fires and chemical reactions.

Any aliens visiting our Solar System could tell Earth was a live planet even without coming here, because it is balanced in a chemically active state. In modern language, it exists on the edge of chaos, in a state of self-organised criticality.

The name Gaia was given to Jim Lovelock's hypothesis by the novelist William Golding (author of *Lord of the Flies*), who was a neighbour of Lovelock and one of the first people he told about the idea.

The whole world – Gaia – runs on the same rules as the sandpile. How much further do these rules extend? Perhaps right into the Universe.

All the stars in the sky are part of a single **galaxy**, called the **Milky Way**. The Milky Way is a big disc, turning around in space.

There are more than 100 billion stars in the Milky Way. They make a spiral pattern, like the cream stirred into a cup of coffee.

The bright spiral 'arms' are places where new stars are born and shine very brightly. As they get older, they get spread around in the disc.

Stars form in the spiral arms because huge clouds of gas moving round the disc get squeezed as they pass through the arms. The cloud collapses and shrinks under its own weight. It breaks up into hot blobs of gas – stars.

But why do the clouds of gas get squeezed in the spiral arms? Because there are a lot of hot, young stars there. The biggest of the new stars do not live very long. Before they move out of the spiral arms, they explode. These explosions, called **supernovas**, squeeze the clouds of gas passing through the arms.

TOO FAST TO LIVE, TOO YOUNG TO DIE

Without this feedback, all the stars in the Milky Way would get spread out evenly round the disc, sit quietly on their own, and gradually fade away. They would be about as interesting as a pile of sand with nothing being added.

But the Milky Way is a dynamic, changing system. It is kept far away from equilibrium, thanks to the input of energy from collapsing clouds and stellar explosions. It only looks stable to us because a star takes hundreds of millions of years to orbit once around the disc. But it seems really to be in a state of self-organised criticality.

HE'S GOING TO BURN HIMSELF OUT

"There seems to be a kind of ecology in the physics of spiral galaxies by means of which the structures responsible for star formation – the spiral arms and associated clouds of dust and gas – are maintained for time scales much longer than the relevant dynamical time scales . . . These must involve self-organizing cycles of materials and energy of the kind that one sees in non-equilibrium states as well as in biological systems."

Professor Lee Smolin,
Syracuse University, USA

Does this mean the Milky Way galaxy is alive? Perhaps it does.

Key dates in the History of Chaos and Uncertainty

1687 Isaac Newton publishes his discovery of the laws on which the Universe operates, in his book *Philosophiae Naturalis Principia Mathematica* (*The Mathematical Principles of Natural Philosophy*, but always known as '*the Principia*').

Mid-1780s Pierre Laplace proves that there is no need for 'the hand of God' to correct the orbits of Jupiter and Saturn. They do it by themselves.

1801 First known asteroid, Ceres, discovered.

1802 Thomas Young proves that light travels as a form of wave.

1859 James Clerk Maxwell proves that the rings of Saturn are made up of many tiny particles, each in its own orbit, like miniature moons.

1859 Charles Darwin publishes his theory of evolution by natural selection.

1875 Henry Smith invents the 'Cantor set.'

1890 Henri Poincare publishes his paper on the 'three body problem.'

1897 J. J. Thomson proves that 'cathode rays' are a stream of tiny particles – electrons.

1903 Poincare spells out the importance of sensitivity to initial conditions.

1905 Albert Einstein proves that the photoelectric effect can be explained if light is a stream of particles.

1923 Louis de Broglie invents the idea of wave-particle duality.

1927 George Thomson (and others) show that electrons travel as a form of wave.

1927 Werner Heisenberg discovers the uncertainty principle.

1961 Edward Lorenz discovers chaos (sensitivity to initial conditions) in weather systems.

Early 1960s Stephen Smale develops the idea of 'attractors'.

Late 1960s Jim Lovelock comes up with the idea of Gaia – the living Earth.

1971 David Ruelle suggests that turbulence is chaotic.

1972 Edward Lorenz invents the term 'butterfly effect.'

1977 Benoit Mandelbrot publishes an influential book about fractals – *The Fractal Geometry of Nature*.

1980s Per Bak and colleagues use the sandpile analogy (model) to investigate self-organised criticality.

1992 Lee Smolin suggests that the Milky Way is a self-organizing system, and may be alive.

Glossary

Asteroid A lump of rock in orbit around the Sun; much smaller than a planet.

Atom The smallest piece of stuff that takes part in chemical reactions. Everything on Earth is made of atoms.

Attractor A pattern of behaviour that systems settle in to.

Billion One thousand million. 1,000,000,000.

Butterfly effect When a small change in where you start has a big effect on where you end up.

Chaos The result of the butterfly effect at work.

Ecology A system of living things in balance with one another. This might be on a small scale (the ecology of a field, or an island), or it might mean the whole of Planet Earth.

Electron Tiny particle which is part of an atom. But it is also a wave!

Extinction When lots of different plants and animals are killed off together.

Feedback When what something does affects its own behaviour.

Fractal A pattern which looks the same as itself when you zoom in on a detail. It is self-similar and scale free.

Gaia Hypothesis The idea that the whole Earth behaves like a single living organism.

Galaxy A huge group of stars in outer space. The Milky Way is a galaxy.

Gravity The force that pulls us down to the surface of the Earth and gives us weight. It also holds the Earth and other planets in orbit around the Sun in the Solar System.

Initial conditions The way something starts out.

Irrational number A number that cannot be written as a fraction (a 'ratio') of two whole numbers. Pi is an irrational number.

Iteration When you do the same thing over and over again.

Law In science, a law is a rule which Nature operates with. Newton's laws tell you exactly where a thing is going, and how fast – but you would need to know exactly how it started to work this out.

Linear When the change in where you end up is proportional to the amount of change in where you started.

Mass Extinction When very many plants and animals are killed off at once.

Milky Way The galaxy in which we live. There are more than 100 billion stars in the Milky Way.

Nonlinear When a small change in where you start makes a big difference to where you end up.

Nucleus The central core of an atom. Electrons move around the nucleus.

Orbit The path followed by a planet (or anything else) going round the Sun, or a moon going round a planet.

Photoelectric effect When light hits a metal and makes electricity.

Photon A particle of light. But light is also a wave!

Power law A mathematical pattern where changing one number changes another number by a certain power.

Punctuated equilibrium When something stays the same for a long time, then suddenly changes and stays in a new state for a long time, then suddenly changes, and so on.

Quantum physics The laws of physics that apply to very small things, like atoms and electrons.

Rational number A number that can be written as a fraction (ratio) using two whole numbers. Numbers like $3/4$ or $15/29$.

Red Queen effect When evolving species have to adapt quickly just to maintain their place in the ecology.

Scale free When something looks the same however you zoom in on it, like a fractal.

Second Law of Thermodynamics The law of nature which says that things wear out, unless energy is used to maintain them.

Solar System The Sun and everything that is in orbit around the Sun.

Self similarity When something is scale free.

Self organisation The way in which a lot of simple things working together use energy to make themselves into something more complicated.

Self-organised criticality When a system maintains itself in an interesting state on the edge of chaos.

Star A hot ball of gas in space that shines because it is hot.

Strange attractor The kind of attractor that produces chaos.

Sun The nearest star, round which the Earth orbits.

Supernova The explosion of a very large star.

System Any collection of things that changes in accordance with the laws of nature – including a sandpile, the Solar System, and even the Milky Way.

Uncertainty There are two kinds of uncertainty in science. Quantum uncertainty says that a thing like an atom simply doesn't have exact properties like a position and a speed, but is kind of fuzzy. The kind of uncertainty important in chaos says there are some things that are not fuzzy, but have to be measured to an infinite number of decimal places in order for their effects to be predicted. That can't be done, no matter how good your measuring equipment is.

Finding out more

Books

Mary and John Gribbin, What's the Big Idea: *Time and the Universe* (Hodder, London, 1997).

Nina Hall (editor), The New Scientist Guide to Chaos (Penguin, London, 1992).

James Lovelock, *Gaia* (Gaia Books, London, 1991).

Ziauddin Sardar and Iwona Abrams, *Chaos for Beginners* (Icon, Cambridge, 1998).

Per Bak, *How Nature Works* (Oxford UP, Oxford, 1997).

James Gleick, *Chaos* (Heinemann, London, 1988).

John Gribbin, *In the Beginning* (Penguin, London, 1994).

Ian Stewart, *Does God Play Dice?* (Blackwell, Oxford, 1989).

Websites

Chaos Club
http://www.chaosclub.com/
An interactive website for young people.

Fractory
http://library.vanced.org/3288/
Design your own fractal.

INDEX

WHAT'S THE BIG IDEA?

Have you read them all?

0 340 72263 0	Alien Life	£3.99 ☐
0 340 66720 6	Animal Rights	£3.99 ☐
0 340 74382 4	Artificial Intelligence	£3.99 ☐
0 340 67847 X	The Environment	£3.99 ☐
0 340 72405 6	Food	£3.99 ☐
0 340 70877 8	Genetics	£3.99 ☐
0 340 72291 6	The Media	£3.99 ☐
0 340 65588 7	The Mind	£3.99 ☐
0 340 69339 8	Nuclear Power	£3.99 ☐
0 340 71482 4	The Paranormal	£3.99 ☐
0 340 66719 2	Religion	£3.99 ☐
0 340 65590 9	Time and the Universe	£3.99 ☐
0 340 65591 7	Virtual Reality	£3.99 ☐
0 340 65589 5	Women's Rights	£3.99 ☐

Turn the page to find out how to order these books.

ORDER FORM

Books in this series are available at your local bookshop, or can be ordered direct from the publisher. A complete list of titles is given on the previous page. Just tick the titles you would like and complete the details below. Prices and availability are subject to change without prior notice.

Please enclose a cheque or postal order made payable to Bookpoint Ltd, and send to: Hodder Children's Books, Cash Sales Dept, Bookpoint, 39 Milton Park, Abingdon, Oxon OX14 4TD.
Email address: orders@bookpoint.co.uk.

If you would prefer to pay by credit card, our call centre team would be delighted to take your order by telephone. Our direct line is 01235 400414 (lines open 9.00 am – 6.00 pm, Monday to Saturday; 24 hour message answering service). Alternatively you can send a fax on 01235 400454.

Title .... First name .... Surname ....

Address ....

....

....

Daytime tel .... Postcode ....

If you would prefer to post a credit card order, please complete the following.

Please debit my Visa/Access/Diners Card/American Express (delete as applicable) card number:

Signature .... Expiry Date ....

If you would NOT like to receive further information on our products, please tick ☐.